Handling Sales Objections with

Mickey's Amazing
Flashcard Learning System

The preferred method of learning
for hundreds of years

Learning 2 Sell LLC
learning2sell.com
mickeymoore@learning2sell.com

ISBN: 978-1-7340966-1-3

Printed in the USA.

Why Flashcards Work

1. Flashcards engage and train your mental faculty known as "active recall". In other words, the repetitive use of flashcards causes your mind to remember a question and quickly recall the answer.

2. Flashcards allow your brain to compare your answer to the correct answer. If you agree with the answer, your mind will accept it as truth and will become ingrained in your mind.

3. Flashcards allow you to study each question separately as needed

Steps to Handling Objections

#1. Hear the objection out

Do exactly that. Relax, let your prospect say whatever they have to say. Don't try to steamroller people with an answer before the question is barely out of their mouth. There are four other steps that can be used prior to your attempt to answer an objection.

Steps to Handling Objections

#2. Feed the objection back to them

Repeat or echo their objection back to them with appropriate voice inflection, loudness, and rate of speaking. It is extremely important to convey your response properly.

For instance, they say "your price is too high." Use inflection or emphasis, on the underscored word, "**our** price is too high?" or "our **price** is to high" or "our price is **too high**?" or "our price is too **high**?"

Many times, your prospect will answer their own objection without going any further, or they may realize that there is no basis for making such a statement. Remember, it's how you say it that counts.

Steps to Handling Objections

#3. Question the objection

Further break down the objection in order to find out what's really on their mind.

For example: "Apparently you have a reason for feeling that way. May I ask what that is?"

#4. Answer the objection with an <u>Empathic Cushion</u>

"I understand how you <u>feel</u>. Many of my best clients <u>felt</u> the same way. This is what they <u>found</u>." Then share with your prospect why your prior clients chose to purchase your product.

#5. Smoke out the objection

"If you weren't concerned about (the objection), then, in your opinion do you feel that you would proceed?" Or "Is there anything else that concerns you before going ahead?"

Steps to Handling Objections

#6. Answer the objection using the following techniques

#6A. Model this purchase after their last purchase.

How long have you been using what you now have? What did you use previously? Did you do a lot of research before you changed? Are your benefits much better now? If you received all these benefits from a previous change, why do you deny yourself now, the opportunity of receiving more benefits by making another change? You did it before.... you can do well again, can't you?"

Steps to Handling Objections

#6B. Changing perspective on what's important to them

Do this by highlighting a major benefit to dwarf the minor objection.

"Is your decision going to be based on a half percent difference in the interest rate, or the total benefit of a tax-free and worry-free return?"

Know your product! Be Creative!

#6C. Deny their logic

Avoid arguments! However, if they should viciously attack you, your company, or your product with a derogatory comment, deny it quickly and emphatically and move on.

Example: "I appreciate your frankness. That comment is concerning to me. I certainly would like to know where you heard something like that about our product. It's currently doing a great job serving our clients' needs and we get many favorable comments regarding it. My professional reputation is based on my professional integrity. I intend to keep it that way by marketing what's right!

Steps to Handling Objections

#6D. Explain the benefits of
your product differently

This is a simple, straight forward explanation to their question. The key word here is simple, because the complex technicalities of your product may bore and confuse your prospect, so getting into detail should be avoided. Just quick & simple.

Steps to Handling Objections

#6E. Use an Analogy

With some thought and creativity, you can come up with a good number of analogies that relate to the situation.

"When you're talking about the Rolls Royce of our industry, what do I really <u>need</u> to say about it?"

OR

"If you were doubling over in pain right now, would you want a doctor with a proven record and who cares for your health or would you want the cheapest guy in town with no concern for your long-term healthcare?"

Steps to Handling Objections

#6F. Put the shoe on their foot

"Let's assume that you are now the President of your organization. What would you do in developing and presenting a product that would serve most everyone? Would you make sure that quality and reliability were built in? Even if it wasn't the least expensive, would you make certain that it had good value for the money? And do you think that standing behind it with great service should be included? Would you want to have a reputation for having many satisfied clients? You see that's exactly what we've done."

Steps to Handling Objections

#6G. Benefit Summary/Question Down

Examples:

- "John, you did say that quality is important, didn't you?"

- "And wouldn't you agree that the tax-saving aspect is vital? "

- "Our reputation for professionalism and a high number of satisfied customers is most favorable. Don't you agree?"

- "You did say that saving time and energy was something you felt imperative. Didn't you?"

- "The increase in confidence and security means a lot to you. Doesn't it?"

Steps to Handling Objections

#6H. Admit it

Admit it, agree with them, and then give about three or four quick benefits of your product.

Example: "You're exactly right. It is a little more costly than others, and in addition to that, it holds its value much better, lasts longer and better performance. Those who bought this are proud to own it!"

Steps to Handling Objections

#7. Confirm the Answer

- "That clarifies this point entirely, don't you agree?"

- "That's what you're looking for, isn't it?"

- "That handles the problem, doesn't it?"

- "That takes care of our concern, doesn't it?"

Steps to Handling Objections

8. Personal Reflection before asking for the sale

- **Personal:** Does the customer seem to like, trust & respect you?

- **Product:** Does the customer think the product will do the job and is of the right quality?

- **Price:** Have you effectively justified the price?

- **Peers:** Has the customer mentioned what others may think of his purchase?

- **Priority:** Does the customer show signs of needing the product now?

Mickey's Amazing Flashcard Learning System

QUESTIONING THE OBJECTION

Objection #1:

Your price is too high

Mickey's Amazing Flashcard Learning System

Question:

How much too high is it?

Mickey's Amazing Flashcard Learning System

Objection #2:

The cost of it is higher than I wanted to go.

Mickey's Amazing Flashcard Learning System

Question:

How much higher is it over what you were thinking about budgeting?

OR

So, in other words what you're saying is, show you why it has extra value for the money and you'll go ahead. Is that correct?

Mickey's Amazing Flashcard Learning System

Objection #3:

I think we'll just stick with what we have.

Question:

**Apparently you have a reason for feeling that way.
May I ask what it is?**

Mickey's Amazing Flashcard Learning System

Objection #4:

Well, I want to think it over.

Question:

So, in other words what you're asking is,
am I making the right decision. Is that correct?

OR

Apparently, you have a reason for feeling that way.
May I ask what that is?

Objection #5:

I've never heard of your company or product.

Question:

So, in other words what you're asking is, can I trust doing business with you. Is that right?

Objection #6:I

We're going to stay with our current supplier.

Mickey's Amazing Flashcard Learning System

Question:

So, in other words what you're saying is, give us more or something better than we're used to getting, and we'll give you the business. Is that right?

Objection #7:

I'm satisfied with where we are.

Question:

So, in other words, what you're saying is, find us a car that I will be just as happy with, with better value, and we'll give it strong consideration. Is that correct?

Mickey's Amazing Flashcard Learning System

Objection #8:

I've had a better offer from another company.

Mickey's Amazing Flashcard Learning System

Question:

So, in other words what you're asking is, what am I getting for the difference in the two offers. Is that right?

Mickey's Amazing Flashcard Learning System

Objection #9:

Well, I think it's a waste of money and a poor investment.

Question:

Apparently, you have a reason for feeling that way.
May I ask what it is?

Objection #10:

I can get it for less.

Question:

So, in other words what you're asking is why should I do business here. Is that right?

Objection #11:

We never make decisions of this magnitude quickly.

Question:

So, in other words what you're asking is, how can I be sure that I'm making the correct decision whether it's today or tomorrow. Is that right?

Objection #12:

We want to sleep on it.

Question:

So, in other words what you're saying is, will sleep help make the decision or will I sleep much better after having made the decision. Is that right?

Mickey's Amazing Flashcard Learning System

Objection #13:

I want to shop around some more. I'll be back or give you a call.

Question:

So, in other words what you're asking is,
can I trust what you have to sell is the best that I can get.
Is that right?

Mickey's Amazing Flashcard Learning System

Objection #14:

I'm over budget now, see me next year.

Mickey's Amazing Flashcard Learning System

Question:

So, in other words what you're saying is, show me how this will increase my profits so that I can expand my working budget, and I'll go ahead. Is that correct?

Mickey's Amazing Flashcard Learning System

Objection #15:

I must talk this over with my accountant or attorney.

Question:

So, in other words what you're saying is, show me how they couldn't possibly say "no" and I would just go ahead and make the decision without wasting that time. Is that correct?

Objection #16:

I just can't afford it.

Question:

So, what you're saying is, show me how I can work it into my budget with easy payments and I'll probably go ahead. Is that right?

Mickey's Amazing Flashcard Learning System

Objection #17:

Thank you for your time.
It was a great presentation, but I'm not interested.

Question:

Apparently you have a reason for feeling that way.
May I ask what it is?

Mickey's Amazing Flashcard Learning System

Objection #18:

This really looks good. I'll let you know.

Question:

So, in other words what you're saying is,
make it look a little better and I'll let you know right now.
Is that correct?

Objection #19:

We don't have the money to pay for it right now.

Question:

So, in other words what you're saying is, show me how I can have it now and start paying for it later and I'll go ahead. Is that right?

Mickey's Amazing Flashcard Learning System

Objection #20:

The board of directors will have to decide on this later.

Question:

So in other words what you're saying is, give me all of the evidence needed for the board to say "yes" and I'll get the ball rolling now. Is that correct?

Objection #21:

We know somebody else in the business. We'll let them handle it for us.

Question:

So, in other words what you're saying is, give us excellent service, be willing to go that extra mile and we'll give you a shot. Is that right?

Objection #22:

I must talk this over with my husband first.

Question:

So, in other words what you're saying is,
show me how my husband will end up with a smile on his
face from my decision instead of a frown and I'll go ahead.
Is that correct?

Objection #23:

My wife and I make joint decisions. I must talk with her.

Question:

So, in other words what you're saying is, show me how to make her really happy and I'll do it for her as a nice surprise. Is that right?

Mickey's Amazing Flashcard Learning System

Objection #24:

I can do better with my own money somewhere else.

Mickey's Amazing Flashcard Learning System

Question:

**Apparently you have a reason for feeling that way.
May I ask what it is?**

64

Objection #25:

I'm going to wait for the interest rates to go down some more.

Question:

So, in other words what you're asking is, will I show you why waiting will hurt me _more_ than doing something now. Is that right?

Mickey's Amazing Flashcard Learning System

Objection #26:

It just came out.
The prices will drop later with competition.

Mickey's Amazing Flashcard Learning System

Question:

So, in other words what you're saying is, show me how I can gain the edge and benefit now while everybody else waits for a possible price drop later. Is that correct?

Mickey's Amazing Flashcard Learning System

Objection #27:

**The economy isn't good.
Now isn't the best time to purchase.**

Mickey's Amazing Flashcard Learning System

Question:

So, in other words what you're saying is, only those people that have made decisions during perfect economic times have been the ones to benefit most. Is that right?

Mickey's Amazing Flashcard Learning System

Objection #28:

I saw something better somewhere else.

Question:

Apparently, you have a reason for feeling that way. May I ask what it is?

Mickey's Amazing Flashcard Learning System

Objection #29:

It's too small for what we want.

Mickey's Amazing Flashcard Learning System

Question:

So, in other words what you're saying is, show me why so many others have benefited from this size. Is that right?

Objection #30:

It's too large for what we want.

Question:

So, in other words what you're saying is, show me how the size can actually work to my advantage. Is that correct?

Mickey's Amazing Flashcard Learning System

Objection #31:

I don't like your range of colors or style.

Question:

So, in other words what you're asking is, why have so many other people found it attractive and desirable. Is that right?

Mickey's Amazing Flashcard Learning System

Objection #32:

Your product hasn't been on the market long enough.

Question:

So, in other words what you're saying is, show me why it's going to be such a huge success in the market. Is that right?

Mickey's Amazing Flashcard Learning System

Objection #33:

I know someone who purchased this and doesn't like it.

Question:

Apparently, they had a reason for feeling that way. May I ask what it is?

Mickey's Amazing Flashcard Learning System

Objection #34:

I heard it breaks down frequently and isn't dependable.

Question:

So, in other words what you're saying is, show me why you have so many satisfied customers. Is that correct?

Mickey's Amazing Flashcard Learning System

Objection #35:

I understand parts are expensive and hard to get.

Mickey's Amazing Flashcard Learning System

Question:

So, in other words what you're saying is, quick service at a reasonable price is important to you. Is that correct?

Objection #36:

You salesman are alike. You'd sell anything to anyone.

Question:

So, in other words what you're asking is, where can I find someone I can trust. Is that right?

Mickey's Amazing Flashcard Learning System

Objection #37:

I'll never see you again when I have problems. No service.

Question:

So, in other words what you're saying is, don't leave me after you sell me and I'll give you my business. Is that right?

Objection #38:

The way this is put together doesn't look too good.

Question:

So, in other words what you're asking is, why was this design and construction chosen to do the job. Is that right?

Objection #39:

We don't have anywhere to put it. There's just no room.

Question:

So, in other words what you're saying is, show me how it's going to do all that you say it will for me and I'll make room for it. Is that right?

Mickey's Amazing Flashcard Learning System

Objection #40:

You're too far away. We want to purchase from someone who is closer to our home.

Question:

So, in other words what you're saying is, just stay on top of us, give us what we want, when we need it, because that's what really counts. Is that correct?